Love Letters of Great Men

~~*

Vol. 1

John C. Kirkland

Love Letters of Great Men
Volume One

Copyright © 2008 John C. Kirkland

www.llogm.com

Library of Congress Cataloging-in-Publication data available upon request

Love letters of great men, volume 1 / compilation and commentary by John C. Kirkland

1. Love-letters. I. Title. Love letters of great men, volume 1. II. Kirkland, John C.

First edition
Published in the United States of America

For her

Table of Contents

Late Nineteenth Century

Twentieth Century

Afterword

List of Illustrations

St. George and the Dragon by
Gustave Moreau (1890)

Foreword

The Poet Warrior

For millennia the poet warrior has been the archetype of the romantic hero. Powerful but sensitive, dangerous but caring, brilliant but misunderstood. From Ulysses to Indiana Jones, every man wants to be him and every woman wants to be with him. Despite the prevalence of this ideal, many believe the poet warrior exists only in the realm of fiction. In truth, as you may glean from reading the compilation of love letters gathered here, some of history's greatest leaders have shown—at least to those they care the most about—that they too have the soul of a poet.

Real men are much more astonishing than avatars. Napoléon is universally known as a superb military tactician, but he also led the archaeological expedition that discovered the ancient Rosetta Stone. The brilliant romantic poet, Lord Byron, commanded the Greek revolutionary forces against the Ottoman Turks. Goethe not only wrote the classic *Faust*, he discovered the intermaxillary bone in the human jaw that inspired Darwin's theory of evolution. The poet warrior is everywhere.

Since before the watchers of the sky created Stonehenge, Khufu conceived the Great Pyramid, or the first farmer toiled in the Céide Fields, closer to the time glacial ice still covered their lands than to today, the fianna of Éire lived as hunters and warriors, men who could be called upon for the protection of the kingdom in time of need. Young nobility who had yet to inherit their land or fortune, these early Gaelic poets survived by hunting for food and furs. Though forced by circumstance to live mostly outside society, they mingled comfortably among aristocrats. One who demonstrated sufficient skill with words, by the telling of tales of honor and glory, recitation of poems of love and loss, or singing of odes of leitmotiv and meditation, may be invited to face the trials and prove his worth to join this druidic coalition of clans.

Hair ceremonially braided he would run a gauntlet of his fellows through the thick forest, a single twig snapping under foot or mere hair out of place resulting in failure. Buried to his waist in peat with only a wooden shield to protect him, the slightest drop of blood caused by any of the nine spears thrust upon him meaning he would never have a chance to help defend the defenseless in battle. At least, that's what they told the ladies that night. Their ancient motto has been adopted by the special forces of the

Army Ranger Wing, the Republic of Ireland's premier hostage rescue unit:

- ❖ Glaine ár gcroí (purity of our hearts)
- ❖ Neart ár ngéag (strength of our limbs)
- ❖ Beart de réir ár mbriathar (deeds to match our words)

History is replete with examples of those who lead by example, with wisdom, courage and love, guided by reflection and empathy, using their minds to accomplish what their hearts know to be true. Tolstoy ended the lives of many men at the end of a cannon or the point of a sword, before writing the words that inspired a generation of nonviolent resistance that changed the world. The legendary stories of the garden of Gethsemane may be the apogee of the poet warrior—simultaneously the highest conceivable levels of both courage and compassion.

Like the Tao, the true poet warrior is subtle and quiescent, circumventing attempts to force his way; simultaneously passionate and indifferent, nurturing and giving wholly of himself to each who comes across his path. Like a first growth Bordeaux he is deep and complex, rich and balanced, dedicated to both the intellect and the corpus, the field of study and the field of battle. He exemplifies the way of the warrior, from the Analects of Confucius and the Bushido code of the Samurai, to the medieval knightly virtues of chivalry, honor and courtly love.

Sir Walter Raleigh gladly suffered the Tower rather than be separated from his true love, and chose to let his head—rather than his honor—be separated from his corporal form. Such greatness often comes with a price, and real men are infinitely more involuted than their fictional counterparts. Greatness may be good or evil, but is more often a combination of both, at least in some measure. Great men and great loves are not caricatures; they are complex, complicated and, often, conflicted. Henry VIII freely professed his love for his wives, but that did not stop him from sometimes taking their lives.

Victory and failure, forgiveness and betrayal, masterwork and bagatelle, it is each poet warrior's individual journey, battles and scars that provide a true glimpse into greatness.

Ovid as portrayed in the *Book of Chronicles* (1493),
one of the earliest printed volumes

First Century

Publius Ovidius Naso

to Fabia

8 A.D.
Tomis, Roman Provinces

I ploughed the vast ocean on a frail bit of timber;
the ship that bore the son of Jason was strong... The
furtive arts of Cupid aided him; arts which I wish that
Love had not learned from me. He returned home; I
shall die in these lands, if the heavy wrath of the
offended God shall be lasting.

My burden, most faithful wife, is a harder one than
that which the son of Jason bore. You, too, whom I

left still young at my departure from the City, I can believe to have grown old under my calamities. Oh, grant it, ye Gods, that I may be enabled to see you, even if such, and to give the joyous kiss on each cheek in its turn; and to embrace your emaciated body in my arms, and to say, "'twas anxiety, on my account, that caused this thinness;" and, weeping, to recount in person my sorrows to you in tears, and thus enjoy a conversation that I had never hoped for; and to offer the due frankincense, with grateful hand, to the Caesars, and to the wife that is worthy of a Caesar, Deities in real truth!

Oh, that the mother of Menon, that Prince being softened, would with her rosy lips, speedily call forth that day.

16 A.D.
Tomis

Lyde was not so dear to Antimachus, nor Bittis so loved by her Philetas, as you, my wife, clinging to my heart, worthy of a happier, but not truer husband.

You are the support on which my ruins rest; if I am still anyone, it is all your gift.

It is your doing that I am not despoiled, stripped bare by those who sought the planks from my shipwreck.

As a wolf raging with the prod of hunger, eager for blood, catches the fold unguarded, or as a greedy vulture peers around to see if it can find an unburied corpse, so someone, faithless, in my bitter trouble, would have come into my wealth, if you had let them.

Your courage, with our friends, drove them off, bravely, friends I can never thank as they deserve.

So you are proven, by one who is as true as he is wretched, if such a witness carries any weight.

Neither Andromache, nor Laodamia, companion of her husband in death, exceeds you in integrity.

If you had been destined for Homer, the Maonian bard, Penelope's fame would be second to yours: either you owe it to your own self, not having been taught loyalty by some teacher, but through the character granted you at birth; or, if it is allowed to compare the small and great, Livia, first lady, honoured by you all those years, teaches you to be the model of a good wife, becoming like her, through long–acquired habit.

Alas, my poetry has no great powers, my lips are inadequate to sing your worth—If I had any innate vigor long ago, it is extinct, quenched by enduring sorrows—or you would be first among the sacred heroines, seen to be first, for the virtues of your heart.

Yet so far as my praise has any power, you will live, for all time, in my verse.

~~*

Publius Ovidius Naso (43 B.C.–17 A.D.), better known as Ovid, was one of the greatest poets of the ancient world. Most remembered for his epic collection of myths and legends, *Metamorphoses*, his writings have had a decisive influence on centuries of Western art and literature.

Ovid was married three times, the first two for financial and political reasons. He was separated from his last wife, Fabia, for the final nine years of his life. In 8 A.D., Augustus banished Ovid to the Greek colony of Tomis, in the province of Scythia Minor on the Black Sea, for "a poem and a mistake" in drawing attention to the scandalous adultery of Ceasar's daughter Julia. During this period of exile in what is now the seaport of Constanța, Romania, Ovid wrote prodigiously.

To illustrate his feelings of epic despair, Ovid makes frequent comparisons to Greek legends, such as Jason and the Argonauts in search of the Golden Fleece, and prior writers, such as Antimachus and Homer. Though addressed to his beloved wife, for whom he continued to pine, the poems were widely read throughout Roman society.

Gaius Plinius Secundus

to Calpurnia

100 A.D.
Rome

You say that you are feeling my absence very much, and your only comfort when I am not there is to hold my writings in your hand and often put them in my place by your side. I like to think that you miss me and find relief in this sort of consolation. I, too, am always reading your letters, and returning to them again and again as if they were new to me—but this only fans the fire of my longing for you. If your letters are so dear to me, you can imagine how I delight in your company; do write as often as you can, although you give me pleasure mingled with pain.

~~*

Gaius Plinius Caecilius Secundus (61–113 A.D.), better known as Pliny the Younger, was a Roman senator, consul and governor, whose famous collection of letters has provided history with the most complete picture available of life at the end of the 1st century.

Pliny was the great-great-grandson of Scipio, the Roman general who defeated Hannibal in the Second Punic War. In 79 A.D., Pliny witnessed the eruption of Mount Vesuvius, which killed his uncle, Pliny the Elder, author of the famous *Naturalis Historia*. A successful attorney, Pliny corresponded with the historian Tacitus, the senator Cicero, and the doctor of the church Saint Augustine. He also delivered a speech in honor of the emperor Trajan.

Pliny had three marriages, the last to Calpurnia, daughter of Roman poet Titus Calpurnius Siculus. They were deeply in love, and saddened when they were unable to have children. Pliny died suddenly while serving as governor in the Roman province of Bithynia–Pontus.

Portrait of King Henry VIII by Hans Holbein
the Younger (1540)

Sixteenth Century

King Henry VIII

to Anne Boleyn

1528
London

My Mistress and Friend,
I and my heart put ourselves in your hands, begging you to recommend us to your good grace and not to let absence lessen your affection...

For myself the pang of absence is already to great, and when I think of the increase of what I must needs suffer it would be well nigh intolerable but for my firm hope of your unchangeable affection...

1528
London

In debating with myself the contents of your letters I have been put to a great agony; not knowing how to understand them, whether to my disadvantage as shown in some places, or to my advantage as in others. I beseech you now with all my heart definitely to let me know your whole mind as to the love between us; for necessity compels me to plague you for a reply, having been for more than a year now struck by the dart of love, and being uncertain either of failure or of finding a place in your heart and affection, which point has certainly kept me for some time from naming you my mistress, since if you only love me with an ordinary love the name is not appropriate to you, seeing that it stands for an uncommon position very remote from the ordinary; but if it pleases you to do the duty of a true, loyal mistress and friend, and to give yourself body and heart to me, who have been, and will be, your very loyal servant (if your rigor does not forbid me), I promise you that not only the name will be due to you, but also to take you as my sole mistress, casting off all others than yourself out of mind and affection, and to serve you only; begging you to make me a complete reply to this my rude letter as to how far and in what I can trust; and if it does not please you to reply in writing, to let me know of some place where I can have it by word of mouth, the which place I will seek out with all my heart. No more for fear of wearying you. Written by the hand of him who would willingly remain yours

HR

~~*

His Majesty King Henry VIII of England (1491–1547), best known for having six wives, was one of the most controversial figures in the English monarchy. Though a practicing Catholic, he struggled with the Holy See, separating the Anglican Church from papal authority and establishing himself as head of the Church of England, resulting in his excommunication. Public outcry and the rampant torture and beheading of resisters led to the beginning of the English Reformation.

When his wife, Catherine of Aragon, was unable to produce a male heir to the throne, Henry relentlessly pursued a young lady in waiting, Anne Boleyn, who initially rejected his advances, saying, "I beseech your highness most earnestly to desist, and to this my answer in good part. I would rather lose my life than my honesty." Unable to secure an annulment from the Pope, Henry divorced Catherine in 1533 and married a pregnant Anne, who was crowned queen consort. Anne gave birth to a daughter.

When she was unable to produce a male heir after several miscarriages, Henry took a new mistress, Jane Seymour. Ironically in light of his own frequent infidelities, Henry falsely accused Anne of adultery for having sex with five men including her own brother, and she was beheaded at the Tower Green.

Ten days later, Henry married Jane, who gave birth to the future Edward VI, but died in childbirth. Henry considered Jane to be his "true" wife for giving him a male heir and was buried next to her at his death. Henry later married Anne, sister of Henry's military ally the protestant Duke of Cleves, but he found her unattractive, referring to her as a "Flanders Mare." The marriage was dissolved and Henry married Anne Boleyn's young cousin, Katherine Howard. The eighteen year old queen had an affair, and was executed. A year later, Henry married wealthy widow Catherine Parr, his final wife.

Henry the Great

to Gabrielle d'Estrées

June 16, 1593
Dreux, France

I have waited patiently for one whole day without news of you; I have been counting the time and that's how it must be. But a second day—I can see no reason for it, unless my servants have grown lazy or been captured by the enemy, for I dare not put the blame on you, my beautiful angel: I am too confident of your affection—which is certainly owing to me, for my love was never greater, nor my desire more urgent; that is why I repeat this refrain in all my letters: come, come, come, my dear love.

Honor with your presence the man who, if only he were free, would go a thousand miles to throw himself at your feet and never move from there. As for what is happening here, we have drained the water from the moat, but our cannons are not going to be in place until Friday when, God willing, I will dine in town.

The day after you reach Mantes, my sister will arrive at Anet, where I will have the pleasure of seeing you every day. I am sending you a bouquet of orange blossoms that I have just received. I kiss the hands of the Viscountess if she is there, and of my good friend, and as for you, my dear love, I kiss your feet a million times.

~~*

His Majesty King Henri IV of France (1553–1610), better known as Henry the Great or good king Henry, was the first Bourbon king of France. Tolerant of both Catholicism and Protestantism, he brought unity to a country deeply torn by religious differences. One of the most popular French kings during and after his reign, Henry showed great concern for the welfare of his subjects. In a line later paraphrased by President Hoover, Henry promised, "God willing, every working man in my kingdom will have a chicken in the pot every Sunday, at the least!"

Gabrielle d'Estrées, daughter of the manipulative and power hungry marquis of Coeuvres, became mistress to Henry in 1591 when she was 18 years of age, and remained so throughout her life. This letter was written from the field before a major battle at Dreux. The Viscountess of the letter is Gabrielle's sister, Francois, and "my good friend" is Henry's sister, Catherine of Bourbon.

Gabrielle had three children by the king, César, Catherine-Henriette and Alexandre, all of whom were legitimized, founding the Vendôme branch of the House of Bourbon. Henry desired to obtain an annulment of his political marriage to his Catholic cousin, Marguerite de Valois, who had failed to produce an heir, and take Gabrielle as his bride, but she unexpectedly died in childbirth at age 26.

Portrait of Sir Walter Raleigh by
Nicholas Hilliard (1585)

Seventeenth Century

Sir Walter Raleigh

to Lady Elizabeth Throckmorton

1603
Tower of London

You shall now receive (my deare wife) my last words in these my last lines. My love I send you that you may keep it when I am dead, and my councell that you may remember it when I am no more. I would not by my will present you with sorrowes (dear Besse) let them go to the grave with me and be buried in the dust. And seeing that it is not Gods will that I should see you any more in this life, beare it patiently, and with a heart like thy selfe.

First, I send you all the thankes which my heart can conceive, or my words can reherse for your many travailes, and care taken for me, which though they have not taken effect as you wished, yet my debt to you is not lesse: but pay it I never shall in this world.

Secondly, I beseech you for the love you beare me living, do not hide your selfe many dayes, but by your travailes seeke to helpe your miserable fortunes and the right of your poor childe. Thy mourning cannot availe me, I am but dust.

Thirdly, you shall understand, that my land conveyed bona fide to my childe: the writings were drawne at midsummer was twelve months, my honest cosen Brett can testify so much, and Dolberry too, can remember somewhat therein. And I trust my blood will quench their malice that have cruelly murthered me: and that they will not seek also to kill thee and thine with extreame poverty.

To what friend to direct thee I know not, for all mine have left me in the true time of tryall. And I perceive that my death was determined from the first day. Most sorry I am God knowes that being thus surprised with death I can leave you in no better estate. God is my witnesse I meant you all my office of wines or all that I could have purchased by selling it, halfe of my stuffe, and all my jewels, but some one for the boy, but God hath prevented all my resolutions. That great God that ruleth all in all, but if you live free from want, care for no more, for the rest is but vanity. Love God, and begin betimes to repose your selfe upon him, and therein shall you finde true and lasting riches, and endlesse comfort: for the rest when you have travailed and wearied your thoughts over all sorts of worldly cogitations, you shall but sit downe by sorrowe in the end.

Teach your son also to love and feare God whilst he is yet young, that the feare of God may grow with him, and then God will be a husband to you, and a father to him; a husband and a father which cannot be taken from you.

Baily oweth me 200 pounds, and Adrian Gilbert 600. In Jersey I also have much owing me besides. The arrearages of the wines will pay my debts. And howsoever you do, for my soules sake, pay all poore men. When I am gone, no doubt you shall be sought for by many, for the world thinkes that I was very rich. But take heed of the pretences of men, and their affections, for they last not but in honest and worthy men, and no greater misery can befall you in this life, than to become a prey, and afterwards to be despised. I speake not this (God knowes) to dissuade you from marriage, for it will be best for you, both in respect of the world and of God. As for me, I am no more yours, nor you mine, death hath cut us asunder: and God hath divided me from the world, and you from me.

Remember your poor childe for his father's sake, who chose you, and loved you in his happiest times. G et those letters (if it be possible) which I writ to the Lords, wherein I sued for my life: God is my witnesse it was for you and yours that I desired life, but it is true that I disdained my self for begging of it: for know it (my deare wife) that your son is the son of a true man, and one who in his owne respect despiseth death and all his misshapen & ugly formes.

I cannot write much, God he knows how hardly I steale this time while others sleep, and it is also time that I should separate my thoughts from the world. Begg my dead body which living was denied thee; and either lay it at Sherburne (and if the land continue) or in Exeter–Church, by my Father and

Mother; I can say no more, time and death call me away.

The everlasting God, powerfull, infinite, and omnipotent God, That Almighty God, who is goodnesse it selfe, the true life and true light keep thee and thine: have mercy on me, and teach me to forgive my persecutors and false accusers, and send us to meet in his glorious Kingdome. My deare wife farewell. Blesse my poore boy. Pray for me, and let my good God hold you both in his armes.

Written with the dying hand of sometimes thy Husband, but now alasse overthrowne.

Yours that was, but now not my own.

Walter Rawleigh

~~*

Sir Walter Raleigh (1552–1618) was a famed English writer, soldier and explorer, and the only Member of Parliament to sit for three counties. A court favorite of Queen Elizabeth I, Raleigh helped colonize the New World, bringing back tobacco and potatoes and publishing an account of his experiences that contributed to the legend of El Dorado.

In 1591, he secretly married one of the Queen's ladies in waiting, Elizabeth Throckmorton, without requesting the Queen's permission, for which he and his new bride were sent to the Tower of London. After being pardoned, they retired to his estate at Sherborne, Dorset.

When Queen Elizabeth died in 1603, Raleigh was arrested and sentenced to death for involvement in the Main Plot against King James I. This letter to Lady Raleigh was written the night before he was to be beheaded, but the following morning he was granted a stay of execution.

Raleigh remained imprisoned in the Tower of London for 15 years, until his release in 1616 to conduct a second expedition in search of the mythical city of gold. He was unsuccessful, and upon his return to England was arrested and beheaded at Whitehall. Raleigh's final words were: "Strike, man, strike!"

Oliver Cromwell

to Elizabeth Cromwell

September 4, 1650
Dunbar, Scotland

For my beloved Wife Elizabeth Cromwell, at the Cockpit:

My Dearest,

I have not leisure to write much, but I could chide thee that in many of thy letters thou writest to me, that I should not be unmindful of thee and thy little ones. Truly, if I love thee not too well, I think I err not on the other hand much. Thou art dearer to me than any creature; let that suffice.

The Lord hath showed us an exceeding mercy: who can tell how great it is. My weak faith hath been upheld. I have been in my inward man marvellously supported; though I assure thee, I grow an old man, and feel infirmities of age marvellously stealing upon me. Would my corruptions did as fast decrease. Pray on my behalf in the latter respect. The particulars of our late success Harry Vane or Gil. Pickering will impart to thee.

My love to all dear friends. I rest thine,

Oliver Cromwell

~~*

Oliver Cromwell (1599–1658) was an English political and military leader who united England, Scotland, Ireland and Wales into a republican Commonwealth. Known as "Old Ironsides" by his troops, he lead the Puritan rebellion that deposed and executed King Charles I in 1649. Loved as a hero of liberty and hated as a nearly genocidal patriot, he radically reformed Parliament and other British institutions, serving as Lord Protector of the commonwealth until his death, when his corpse was dug up, hung in chains and beheaded by the returning Royalists. He married his wife Elizabeth when he was 21 and they remained together throughout his life.

Frontispiece from *Dictionnaire philosophique*
by Voltaire (1764)

Eighteenth Century

Voltaire

to Catherine Dunoyer

1713
The Hague

I am a prisoner here in the name of the King; they can take my life, but not the love that I feel for you. Yes, my adorable mistress, tonight I shall see you, even if I have to put my head on the block to do it.

For heaven's sake, do not speak to me in such disastrous terms as you write; you must live, and be cautious; beware of madame your mother as of your worst enemy. What do I say? Beware of everybody;

trust no one; keep yourself in readiness, as soon as the moon is visible; I shall leave the hotel incognito, take a carriage or a chaise, we will drive like the wind to Sheveningen; I will take paper and ink with me; we will write our letters.

If you love me, reassure yourself; and call all your strength and presence of mind to your aid; do not let your mother notice anything, try to bring your pictures, and be assured that the menace of the greatest tortures will not prevent me from serving you. No, nothing has the power to part me from you; our love is based upon virtue, and will last as long as our lives. Adieu, there is nothing that I will not brave for your sake; you deserve much more than that. Adieu, my dear heart

Arout

~~*

François-Marie Arouet (1694–1778), better known as Voltaire, was a prolific writer and philosopher of the French Enlightenment, most remembered for his radical defense of civil liberties and religious freedom, whose works and ideas helped lead to the French and American Revolutions.

After studying law, Voltaire went to work in the Netherlands as secretary to the French ambassador. There, he met and fell in love with a beautiful French refugee, Catherine Olympe Dunoyer. Their parents disapproved of the scandal and kept the young lovers locked up to keep them apart. Their planned elopement was foiled by his father and Voltaire was forced to return to France.

George Washington

to Martha Washington

May 1775
Philadelphia

It has been determined in Congress, that the whole army raised for the defence of the American cause shall be put under my care, and that it is necessary for me to proceed immediately to Boston to take upon me the command of it.

You may believe me, my dear Patsy, when I assure you in the most solemn manner that, so far from seeking this appointment, I have used every endeavor in my power to avoid it, not only from my unwillingness to part with you and the family, but from a consciousness of its being a trust too great for my capacity, and that I should enjoy more real happiness in one month with you at home than I have the most distant prospect of finding abroad....

It was utterly out of my power to refuse this appointment, without exposing my character to such censure as would have reflected dishonor upon myself, and have given pain to my friends....

I shall rely, therefore, confidently on that Providence which has heretofore preserved and been bountiful to me, not doubting but that I shall return safe to you in the Fall.

~~*

General George Washington (1732–1799), widely considered the father of our country, was commander-in-chief of the Continental Army, which he led to victory over the British in the American Revolutionary War. He then presided over the

Constitutional Convention, and was unanimously elected the first President of the United States, lauded as "first in war, first in peace, and first in the hearts of his countrymen."

Washington met and promptly married Martha Dandridge Custis—a wealthy widow with two children—when they were both twenty-seven years old, and moved the family to his Virginia plantation with over 100 slaves. As a large landowner and local military hero from the French and Indian war, he was elected a delegate to the Second Continental Congress, which appointed him to lead the revolutionary forces.

Weary of politics, he finally retired to his beloved Mount Vernon at the end of his second term as President. He died a mere three years later, bled to death by his physicians attempting to treat an infection. Though she was the nation's first First Lady, Martha was known during her life simply as Lady Washington.

Portrait of Goethe by Johann Heinrich
Wilhelm Tischbein (1788)

Johann Wolfgang von Goethe

to Charlotte von Stein

June 17, 1784
Weimar, Germany

My letters will have shown you how lonely I am. I do not dine at Court, I see few people, and take my walks alone, and at every beautiful spot I wish you were there.

I cannot help loving you more than is good for me; I shall feel all the happier when I see you again. I am always conscious of my closeness to you, your presence never leaves me. In you I have a measure for every woman, for everyone; in your love a measure for all that is to be. Not in the sense that the rest of the world seems obscure to me, on the contrary, your love makes it clear; I see quite clearly what men are like and what they plan, wish, do and enjoy; I do not begrudge them what they have, and comparing is a secret joy to me, possessing as I do such an imperishable treasure.

You in your household must feel as I often do in my affairs; we often do not notice things simply because we do not choose to look at them, but things acquire an interest as soon as we see clearly the way they are related to one another. For we always like to join in, and the good man takes pleasure in arranging, putting in order and fostering the right and its peaceful rule. Farewell, you whom I love a thousand times.

~~*

Johann Wolfgang von Goethe (1749–1832) was one of Germany's greatest writers and the first literary celebrity. Most remembered for his magnum opus, *Faust*, a pinnacle of world literature, he was also an accomplished scientist, whose work influenced Charles Darwin and inspired generations of Western philosophers.

In 1775, Goethe met and fell deeply in love with his muse, Charlotte von Stein, who became the inspiration for the leading female characters in his works.

Robert Burns

to Jean Armour

Summer 1784
Mauchline, Scotland

Dear Madam,

The passion of love has need to be productive of much delight; as where it takes thorough possession of the man, it almost unfits him for anything else.

The lover who is certain of an equal return of affection, is surely the happiest of men; but he who is a prey to the horrors of anxiety and dreaded disappointment, is a being whose situation is by no means enviable.

Of this, my present experience gives me much proof.

To me, amusement seems impertinent, and business intrusion, while you alone engross every faculty of my mind.

May I request you to drop me a line, to inform me when I may wait upon you?

For pity's sake, do; and let me have it soon.

In the meantime allow me, in all the artless sincerity of truth, to assure you that I truly am,

my dearest Madam,

your ardent lover, and devoted humble servant

~~*

Robert Burns (1759–1796), better known simply as The Bard, is widely regarded as the national poet of Scotland. A pioneer of the Romantic movement and inspiration to the founders of liberalism and socialism, he is most remembered for his New Year's poem *Auld Lang Syne*, or once upon a time, set to the tune of a traditional Scottish folksong. (Interestingly, in Scottish, "syne" is pronounced with an "s," not like a "z" as many English speakers commonly pronounce it.)

Burns had many scandalous love affairs, and an illegitimate daughter by his mother's servant. Then he met Jean Armour, the young daughter of a local stonemason. After a brief affair with Mary Campbell, Burns and Jean had twins in 1786 and were married two years later. Known as the Belle of Mauchline, she inspired many of his poems.

Portrait of Leopold, Wolfgang and Anne Maria
Mozart by Louis Carrogis Carmontelle (1764)

Wolfgang Amadeus Mozart

to Constanze Mozart

September 30, 1790
Frankfurt, Germany

Dearest little Wife of my heart!

If only I had a letter from you, everything would be all right.—I hope you received my letter from Efferding and one from Frankfurt.—I told you in my last letter to talk to Ribisel Face;—I would prefer it, just to be on the safe side, if I could raise 2,000 gulden on the draft by H...—but you'd have to give some other reason, for example, that I have some business deal in mind, but you don't know exactly what.—Dearest, I have no doubt that I shall get something going here, but it won't be easy as you and some of our friends think.—It is true, I am known and respected here; but, well—No—let us just see what happens.—In any case, I do prefer to play it safe, that why I would like to conclude this deal with H... because I would get some money into my possession without having to pay any out; all I would have to do then is work, and I shall be only too happy to do that for my little wife.—When you write to me, always address your letter: General delivery.—...

Since I don't know whether you are in Vienna or Baden at present, I'm addressing this letter to Madame Hofer. I get all excited like a child when I think about being with you again—If people could see into my heart I should almost feel ashamed. Everything is cold to me—ice-cold.—If you were here with me, maybe I would find the courtesies people are showing me more enjoyable,—but as it is, it's all so empty—adieu—my dear—I am Forever

your Mozart who loves you
with his entire soul.

October 17, 1790
Mainz, Germany

PS.—while I was writing the last page, tear after tear fell on the paper. But I must cheer up—catch— An astonishing number of kisses are flying about— The deuce!—I see a whole crowd of them. Ha! Ha!...I have just caught three—They are delicious— You can still answer this letter, but you must address your reply to Linz, General Delivery—That is the safest course. As I do not yet know for certain whether I shall go to Regensburg, I can't tell you anything definite. Just write on the cover that the letter is to be kept until called for.

Adieu—Dearest, most beloved little wife—Take care of your health—and don't think of walking into town. Do write and tell me how you like our new quarters—Adieu. I kiss you millions of times.

~~*

Johann Chrysostom Wolfgang Amadeus Mozart (1756–1791) was one of the most prolific and enduringly popular composers in Classical music. A child prodigy, he began touring Europe as a virtuoso pianist at the tender age of five. He wrote hundreds of works including symphonies, concertos, quartets and operas such as *Marriage of Figaro, Don Giovanni,* and *The Magic Flute.*

Mozart befriended the musically talented Weber family when he visited the musical center of Mannheim, and unsuccessfully courted the eldest sister, Aloysia, a professional singer. Years later, Mozart moved in with the family as a lodger in

Vienna, and turned his attentions toward the youngest sister, Constanze, then a nineteen year old professional soprano singer. They began courting and, after a brief breakup when Constance permitted another man to measure her calves in a parlor game, were married and had two surviving sons. She sang the lead aria in the 1783 premiere of his *Mass in C Minor* in Salzburg, and inspired many of his compositions in the Baroque style she loved.

The H in Mozart's letter refers to music publisher Franz Anton Hoffmeister, while Madame Hofer refers to Constanze's sister, Josepha. Mozart died in 1791, leaving his widow and their young children in considerable debt. Constanze was able to find financial security for her family by organizing memorial concerts and publishing her late husband's works. She eventually remarried a Danish diplomat, whom she first met as her lodger.

Napoléon Crossing the St. Bernard Pass
by Jacques-Louis David (1805)

Napoléon Bonaparte

to Joséphine de Beauharnais

December 1795
Paris

I awake consumed with thoughts of you. Your image and the memory of the intoxicating pleasures of last evening have left my senses in turmoil. Sweet, incomparable Josephine, what a strange effect you have on my heart. Are you angry? Do I see you looking sad? Are you worried?... My soul aches with sorrow, and there can be no rest for your lover; but is there still more in store for me when, yielding to the profound feelings that overwhelm me, I draw from your lips, from your heart a love which consumes me with fire? Ah! It was last night that I fully realized how false an image of you your portrait gives!

You are leaving at noon; I shall see you in three hours.

Until then, my sweet love, a thousand kisses; but give me none in return, for they set my blood on fire.

Spring 1797
Cisalpine Republic, Northern Italy

To Joséphine,

I love you no longer; on the contrary, I detest you. You are a wretch, truly perverse, foolish Cinderella. You never write me; you do not love your husband; you know what pleasures your letters give him yet you cannot even manage to write him half a dozen lines, dashed off in a moment! What then do you do all day, Madame? What business is so vital that it robs you of the time to write to your devoted lover?

What affection stifles and pushes aside the love, the tender constant love you promised him? Who can this wonderful new lover be who takes up your every moment, rules your days and prevents your giving any attention to your husband?

Beware, Josephine; one fine night the doors will be broken down and there I will be. In truth, I am worried, my love, at receiving no news of you; write me quickly four pages, pages of those delightful words that will fill my heart with emotion and joy. I hope to hold you in my arms before long, and cover you with a million kisses, burning as the equatorial sun.

~~*

Napoléone di Buonaparte (1769–1821) was a general during the French Revolution who made himself Napoléon I, Emperor of France, Italy, Switzerland and Germany. Widely regarded as one of the greatest military commanders in history, his victorious campaigns against almost every major European power remain required learning at military academies throughout the world. His tactics could be brutal, sometimes killing civilians, prisoners and even his own wounded. He also established the Napoleonic code, the foundations for the French legal system, and was a member of the French Academy of Sciences, leading an expedition to Egypt that discovered the Rosetta Stone.

Weeks after his first command victory in Paris in October 1795, Napoléon met Joséphine de Beauharnais, a prodigal widow six years older than he. They married in March the following year, days before Bonaparte marched on Italy. Within a year Joséphine had an affair with a young cavalry officer, infuriating Bonaparte. By the next year, he had begun having affairs of his own, and their relationship was never the same.

In 1804 they were crowned Emperor and Empress, but Joséphine was unable to produce an heir and by 1810 they were divorced. Napoléon married the eighteen year old Archduchess Maria Luisa of Austria, who bore him a son, Napoléon II. They remained married the rest of his life, though she did not join him in exile following his defeat. Napoléon's final words on the Island of St. Helena were, "France, the Army, the Head of the Army, Joséphine."

Portrait of Ludwig von Beethoven by Christian
Hornemann (1803)

Early Nineteenth Century

Beethoven

to Antonie von Birkenstock Brentano

1812
Teplitz, Bohemia

July 6, in the morning
My angel, my all, my very self—only a few words
today and at that with pencil (yours)—not till
tomorrow will my lodgings be definitely determined
upon—what a useless waste of time. Why this deep
sorrow where necessity speaks—can our love endure
except through sacrifices—through not demanding
everything from one another—can you change it that

you are not wholly mine, I not wholly thine? Oh God!, look out into the beauties of nature and comfort your heart with that which must be—love demands everything and that very justly—thus it is to me with you, and to you with me. But you forget so easily that I must live for me and for you; if we were wholly united you would feel the pain of it as little as I—My journey was a fearful one; I did not reach here until 4 o'clock yesterday morning. Lacking horses the post-coach chose another route, but what an awful one; at the stage before the last I was warned not to travel at night; I was made fearful of a forest, but that only made me the more eager—and I was wrong. The coach must break down on the wretched road, a bottomless mud road. Without such postilions as I had with me I should have remained stuck in the road. Esterhazy, traveling the usual road here, had the same fate with eight horses that I had with four— Yet I got some pleasure out of it, as I always do when I successfully overcome difficulties—Now a quick change to things internal from things external. We shall surely see each other; moreover, today I cannot share with you the thoughts I have had during these last few days touching my own life—if our hearts were always close together I would havee none of these. My heart is full of many things to say to you—ah!—there are moments when I feel that speech is nothing after all—cheer up—remain my true, my only treasure, my all as I am yours; the gods must send us the rest, that for us must and shall be—
Your faithful Ludwig

Evening, Monday, July 6
You are suffering, my dearest creature—only now have I learned that letters must be posted very early in the morning on Mondays to Thursdays—the only days on which the mail-coach goes from here to

Karlsbad—You are suffering—Ah, wherever I am, there you are also—I will arrange it with you and me that I can live with you. What a life, thus, without you—pursued by the goodness of mankind hither and thither—which I as little want to deserve as I deserve it—Humility of man towards man—it pains me—and when I consider myself in relation to the universe, what am I and what is He—whom we call the greatest—and yet—herein lies the divine in man—I weep when I reflect that you will probably not receive the first report from me until Saturday— Much as you love me—I love you more—But do not ever conceal yourself from me—good night—As I am taking the baths I must go to bed—Oh God—so near, so far! Is not our love truly a heavenly structure, and also as firm as the vault of heaven?

Good morning, on July 7
    Though still in bed, my thoughts go out to you, my Immortal Beloved, now and then joyfully, then sadly, waiting to learn whether or not fate will hear us—I can live only wholly with you or not at all—Yes, I am resolved to wander so long away from you until I can fly into your arms and say that I am really at home with you, and can send my soul enwrapped in you into the land of spirits—Yes, unhappily it must be so—You will be the more contained since you know my fidelity to you. No one else can ever possess my heart—never—never—Oh God, why must one be parted from one whom one so loves. And yet my life in Vienna is now a wretched life— Your love makes me at once the happiest and the unhappiest of men—At my age I need a steady, quiet life—can that be so in our connection? My angel, I have just been told that the mailcoach goes every day—therefore I must close at once so that you may receive the letter at once—Be calm, only by a calm

consideration of our existence can we achieve our purpose to live together—Be calm—love me— today—yesterday—what tearful longings for you— you—you—my life—my all—farewell. Oh continue to love me—never misjudge the most faithful heart of your beloved.

ever thine
ever mine
ever ours

~~*

Ludwig van Beethoven (1770–1827) was a German virtuoso pianist and composer, the first with popularity so far beyond the nobility that he became a true public figure within his lifetime. Even while slowly becoming deaf, he continued to conduct, perform, and compose masterpieces. He was a dominant force in the transition from the classical to the romantic era, and his genius had profound influence on later generations of music.

Antonie von Birkenstock Brentano was a twenty-five year old wife and mother of two children when she was introduced to Beethoven by his half sister in 1811. She was married to a Frankfurt banker, who befriended Beethoven while the family was staying in Vienna to settle her father's estate. Beethoven dedicated musical compositions to Antonie and her daughter, and wrote the song cycle *To the Distant Beloved* for her.

Beethoven never married, though he was later engaged to his student, Countess Giulietta Guiccardi, whose parents would not permit them to be married. The letter to his Immortal Beloved was found among Beethoven's personal effects when he died fifteen years after it was written, meaning that it was never sent or was returned by his paramour.

Portrait of George Gordon, Sixth Lord Byron
by Thomas Phillips (1809)

Lord Byron

to Lady Caroline Lamb

August 1812
London

My dearest Caroline,

If tears, which you saw & know I am not apt to shed, if the agitation in which I parted from you, agitation which you must have perceived through the whole of this most nervous nervous affair, did not commence till the moment of leaving you approached, if all that I have said & done, & am still but too ready to say & do, have not sufficiently proved what my real feelings are & must be ever towards you, my love, I have no other proof to offer.

God knows I wish you happy, & when I quit you, or rather when you from a sense of duty to your husband & mother quit me, you shall acknowledge the truth of what I again promise & vow, that no other in word or deed shall ever hold the place in my affection which is & shall be most sacred to you, till I am nothing.

I never knew till that moment, the madness of—my dearest & most beloved friend—I cannot express myself—this is no time for words—but I shall have a pride, a melancholy pleasure, in suffering what you yourself can hardly conceive—for you do not know me.—I am now about to go out with a heavy heart, because—my appearing this evening will stop any absurd story which the events of today might give rise to—do you think now that I am cold & stern, & artful—will even others think so, will your mother even—that mother to whom we must indeed sacrifice much, more much more on my part, than she shall ever know or can imagine.

"Promises not to love you" ah Caroline it is past promising—but shall attribute all concessions to the proper motive—& never cease to feel all that you have already witnessed—& more than can ever be known but

to my own heart—perhaps to yours—May God protect forgive & bless you—ever & even more than ever.

yr. most attached
BYRON

P.S.—These taunts which have driven you to this—my dearest Caroline—were it not for your mother & the kindness of all your connections, is there anything on earth or heaven would have made me so happy as to have made you mine long ago? & not less now than then, but more than ever at this time—you know I would with pleasure give up all here & all beyond the grave for you—& in refraining from this—must my motives be misunderstood—? I care not who knows this—what use is made of it—it is you & to you only that they owe yourself, I was and am yours, freely & most entirely, to obey, to honour, love—& fly with you when, where, & how you yourself might & may determine.

to Countess Teresa Guicciolo

1819
Ravenna, Italy

My dearest Teresa,
I have read this book in your garden, my love, you were absent, or else I could not have read it.
It is a favorite book of mine. You will not understand these English words, and others will not

understand them, which is the reason I have not scrawled them in Italian.

But you will recognize the handwriting of him who passionately loved you, and you will divine that, over a book that was yours, he could only think of love.

In that word, beautiful in all languages, but most so in yours—Amor mio—is comprised my existence here and thereafter.

I feel I exist here, and I feel that I shall exist hereafter, to what purpose you will decide; my destiny rests with you, and you are a woman, eighteen years of age, and two out of a convent, I wish you had stayed there, with all my heart, or at least, that I had never met you in your married state.

But all this is too late. I love you, and you love me, at least, you say so, and act as if you did so, which last is a great consolation in all events.

But I more than love you, and cannot cease to love you. Think of me, sometimes, when the Alps and ocean divide us, but they never will, unless you wish it.

~~*

George Gordon (1788–1824), the 6th Lord Byron, was an English poet widely regarded as among Europe's best, most remembered for romantic works such as his magnum opus, *Don Juan*. He was also a revolutionary leader of the Carbonari—a secret society that helped unify the nation of Italy—and is venerated as a national hero in Greece for fighting against the Ottoman Empire in the Greek war of independence. He was infamous in his time for his wild living, travels, adventures, and many love affairs. As noted by Lady Caroline, he was, "mad, bad, and dangerous to know."

Lady Caroline Lamb was the twenty-seven year old estranged wife of the Prime Minister of England when she began a scandalous affair with Byron in 1812. Initially obsessed with her, Byron eventually ended the relationship, devastating Caroline who stopped eating. Her dogged pursuit caused Byron to remark cruelly that he was being "haunted by a skeleton," and to write a poem that began "Remember thee," and ended, "Thou false to him, thou fiend to me."

Countess Teresa Guicciolo, though only nineteen, was married to a man in his late fifties when Byron met and immediately fell madly in love with her in 1819. Tolerated by her husband and befriended by her father and brother, he lived happily with Teresa for four years. Byron eventually grew restless and travelled to Greece to take command of the elite Souliot soldiers. Caught in a storm he fell ill, and was bled to death by his treating physicians, dying in Messolonghi in the Spring of 1824.

John Keats

to Fanny Brawne

May 1820
Rome

Tuesday Morn.
My dearest Girl,

I wrote a letter for you yesterday expecting to have seen your mother. I shall be selfish enough to send it though I know it may give you a little pain, because I wish you to see how unhappy I am for love of you, and endeavor as much as I can to entice you to give up your whole heart to me whose whole existence hangs upon you.

You could not step or move an eyelid but it would shoot to my heart—I am greedy of you—Do not think of any thing but me. Do not live as if I was not existing—Do not forget me—But have I any right to say you forget me? Perhaps you think of me all day.

Have I any right to wish you to be unhappy for me? You would forgive me for wishing it, if you knew the extreme passion I have that you should love me—and for you to love me as I do you, you must think of no one but me, much less write that sentence. Yesterday and this morning I have been haunted with a sweet vision—

I have seen you the whole time in your shepherdess dress. How my senses have ached at it! How my heart has been devoted to it! How my eyes have been full of tears at it! Indeed I think a real Love is enough to occupy the widest heart—Your going to town alone, when I heard of it was a shock to me—yet I expected it—promise me you will not for some time, till I get better. Promise me this and fill the paper full of the most endearing names.

If you cannot do so with good will, do my Love tell me—say what you think—confess if your heart is too much fasten'd on the world. Perhaps then I may see you at a greater distance, I may not be able to appropriate you so closely to myself.

Were you to loose a favorite bird from the cage, how would your eyes ache after it as long as it was in sight; when out of sight you would recover a little. Perhaps, if you would, if so it is, confess to me how many things are necessary to you besides me. I might be happier, by being less tantalized.

Well may you exclaim, how selfish, how cruel, not to let me enjoy my youth! To wish me to be unhappy! You must be so if you love me—upon my Soul I can be contented with nothing else. If you could really what is called enjoy yourself at a Party— if you can smile in peoples faces, and with them to admire you now, you never have nor ever will love me—I see life in nothing but the certainty of your Love—convince me of it my sweetest. If I am not somehow convinced I shall die of agony.

If we love me must not live as other men and women do—I cannot brook the wolfsbane of fashion and foppery and tattle. You must be mine to die upon the rack if I want you.

I do not pretend to say I have more feeling than my fellows—but I wish you seriously look over my letters kind and unkind and consider whether the Person who wrote them can be able to endure much longer the agonies and uncertainties of which you are so peculiarly made to create—My recovery of bodily health will be of no benefit to me if you are not all mine when I am well.

For god's sake save me—or tell me my passion is of too awful a nature for you. Again God bless you.
J.K.

No—my sweet Fanny—I am wrong. I do not want you to be unhappy—and yet I do. I must while there is so sweet a Beauty—my loveliest my darling! Good bye! I kiss you—O the torments!

~~*

John Keats (1795–1821) was a young English romantic poet, much criticized in his time, but who has grown to posthumous acclaim, most remembered for his masterwork odes, especially *Ode on a Grecian Urn*.

After losing his brother to consumption in 1818, Keats moved to Hampstead next door to Fanny Brawne, and the two quickly fell deeply in love. Within two years Keats began to succumb to tuberculosis and had to move to a warmer Mediterranean climate. He and Fanny corresponded frequently before his death the following year at twenty-six, and the posthumous publication of his letters to her would create a scandal. Keats was buried in Rome beneath a tombstone reading, "Here lies one whose name was writ in water."

Cosette by Emile Bayard, from the original edition of
Les Misérables by Victor Hugo (1862)

Victor Hugo

to Adèle Foucher

1821
Paris

My dearest,

When two souls, who have sought each other for however long in the throng, have finally found each other... a union, fiery and pure as they themselves are... begins on earth and continues forever in heaven.

This union is love, true love,... a religion, which deifies the loved one, whose life comes from devotion and passion, and for whom the greatest sacrifices are the sweetest delights.

This is the love that you inspire in me... Your soul is made to love with the purity and passion of angels; but perhaps it can only love another angel, in which case I must tremble with apprehension.

Yours forever,
Victor Hugo

Friday evening, March 15, 1822.

After the two delightful evenings spent yesterday and the day before, I certainly will not go out tonight, but will sit here at home and write to you. Besides, my Adele, my adorable and adored Adele, what have I not to tell you? O, God! for two days, I have been asking myself every moment if such happiness is not a dream. It seems to me that what I feel is not of earth. I cannot yet comprehend this cloudless heaven.

You do not yet know, Adele, to what I had resigned myself. Alas, do I know it myself? Because I was weak, I fancied I was calm; because I was preparing myself for all the mad follies of despair, I thought I was courageous and resigned. Ah! let me cast myself humbly at your feet, you who are so grand, so tender and powerful! I had been thinking that the utmost limit of my devotion could only be the sacrifice of my life; but you, my generous love, were ready to sacrifice for me the repose of yours.

...You have been privileged to receive every gift from nature, you have both fortitude and tears. Oh, Adele, do not mistake these words for blind enthusiasm—enthusiasm for you has lasted all my life, and increased day by day. My whole soul is yours. If my entire existence had not been yours, the harmony of my being would have been lost, and I must have died—died inevitably.

These were my meditations, Adele, when the letter that was to bring me hope or else despair arrived. If you love me, you know what must have been my joy. What I know you may have felt, I will not describe.

My Adele, why is there no word for this but joy? Is it because there is no power in human speech to express such happiness? The sudden bound from mournful resignation to infinite felicity seemed to upset me. Even now I am still beside myself and sometimes I tremble lest I should suddenly awaken from this dream divine.

Oh, now you are mine! At last you are mine! Soon—in a few months, perhaps, my angel will sleep in my arms, will awaken in my arms, will live there. All your thoughts at all moments, all your looks will be for me; all my thoughts, all my moments, all my looks, will be for you, my Adele!

Adieu, my angel, my beloved Adele! Adieu! I will kiss your hair and go to bed. Still I am far from you, but I can dream of you. Soon perhaps you will be at my side. Adieu; pardon the delirium of your husband who embraces you, and who adores you, both for this life and another.

~~*

Victor-Marie Hugo (1802–1885) was a French lyric poet, playwright and novelist, most remembered for his masterpieces, *The Hunchback of Notre Dame* and *Les Misérables*, which drew attention to the plight of the working class. He remains one of the most celebrated figures in romantic French literature.

Hugo fell in love with the girl next door, Adèle Foucher, his childhood neighbor. Though madly in love and secretly engaged by their late teens, his mother forbid the relationship, desiring a daughter-in-law with a more formidable pedigree. For three years the two exchanged secret messages. Finally married after his mother's death in 1822, Adèle bore him five children and—despite several affairs by each—the two remained married until her death in 1868.

Franz Liszt

to Countess Marie d'Agoult

July 1834
Paris

My heart overflows with emotion and joy! I do not
know what heavenly languor, what infinite pleasure
permeates it and burns me up. It is as if I had never
loved! Tell me whence these uncanny disturbances
spring, these inexpressible foretastes of delight, these
divine, tremors of love. Oh! all this can only spring
from you, sister, angel, woman, Marie! All this can
only be, is surely nothing less than a gentle ray
streaming from your fiery soul, or else some secret
poignant teardrop which you have long since left in
my breast.

My God, my God, never force us apart, take pity
on us! But what am I saying? Forgive my weakness,
how couldst Thou divide us! Thou wouldst have
nothing but pity for us... No no! It is not in vain that
our flesh and our souls quicken and become immortal
through Thy Word, which cries out deep within us
Father, Father... out Thy hand to us, that our broken
hearts seek their refuge in Thee... O! we thank, bless
and praise Thee, O God, for all that Thou has given
us, and all that Thou hast prepared for us....

This is to be—to be!

Marie! Marie!

Oh let me repeat that name a hundred times, a
thousand times over; for three days now it has lived
within me, oppressed me, set me afire. I am not
writing to you, no, I am close beside you. I see you, I
hear you. Eternity in your arms... Heaven, Hell,
everything, all is within you, redoubled... Oh! Leave
me free to rave in my delirium. Drab, tame,

constricting reality is no longer enough for me. We must live our lives to the full, loving and suffering to extremes!...
Franz

~~*

Ferenc Liszt (1811–1886) was a renowned and influential Hungarian romantic composer and virtuoso pianist. With his exceptional artistry, technical ability, stage presence, and dramatic flair, he is widely regarded as the greatest pianist in history.

In the audience for one of his legendary performances at the Paris apartment of Frédéric Chopin was Marie de Flavigly, the Countess d'Agoult, a rich and beautiful but deeply troubled young wife and mother, who was instantly attracted to the twenty-two year old star. She was also a gifted singer and amateur pianist and the two often played together at Parisian soirées.

After many months of flirtation, intimate correspondence, and public rumor, the two consummated their affair. They lived together for four years and had three children. Their relationship became strained and Liszt spent eight years traveling Europe, performing and having affairs, returning to Marie and his children for the summer holidays before the relationship finally ended in 1844.

The Scarlet Letter by T.H. Matteson (1860)

Nathaniel Hawthorne

to Sophie Peabody

September 23, 1839
Boston

Belovedest little wife—sweetest Sophie Hawthorne—what a delicious walk that was, last Thursday! It seems to me, now, as if I could really remember every footstep of it. It is almost as distinct as the recollection of those walks, in which my earthly form did really tread beside your own, and my arm uphold you; and, indeed, it has the same character as those heavenly ramblings—for did we tread on earth even then?

Oh no—our souls went far away among the sunset clouds, and wherever there was ethereal beauty, there were we, our true selves; and it was there that we grew into each other, and became a married pair.

Dearest, I love to date our marriage as far back as possible; and I feel sure that the tie had been formed, and our union had become indissoluble, even before we sat down together on the steps of the "house of spirits." How beautiful and blessed those hours appear to me!

True; we are far more conscious of our relation, and therefore infinitely happier, now, than we were then; but still those remembrances are among the most precious treasures of my soul.

It is not past happiness; it makes a portion of our present bliss. And thus, doubtless, even amid the Joys of Heaven, we shall love to look back at our earthly bliss, and treasure it forever in the sum of our infinitely accumulating happiness.

Perhaps not a single pressure of the hand, not a glance, not a sweet and tender tone, not one kiss, but will be repeated sometime or other in our memory.

Oh, dearest blessed Dove, I never felt sure of going to Heaven, till I knew that you loved me; but now I am conscious of God's love in your own. And now good bye for a little while, mine own wife. I thought it was just on the verge of supper-time when I began to write—and there is the bell now. I was beginning to fear that it had rung unheard, while I was communining with my Dove. Should we be the more ethereal if we did not eat? I have a most human and earthly appetite. Mine own wife, since supper I have been reading over again (for the third time, the two first being aboard my salt ship—Marcia Cleaves) your letter of yesterday—and a dearest letter it is—and meeting with Sophie Hawthorne twice, I took the liberty to kiss her very fervently. Will she forgive me? Do know yourself by that name, dearest, and think of yourself as Sophie Hawthorne. It thrill my heart to write it, and still more, I think, to read it in the fairy letters of your own hand.

Oh, you are my wife, my dearest, truest, tenderest, most beloved wife. I would not be disjoined from you for a moment, for all the world. And how strong, while I write, is the consciousness that I am truly your husband!

Dove, come to my bosom—it yearns for you as it never did before. I shall fold my arms together, after I am in bed, and try to imagine that you are close to my heart. Naughty wife, what right have you to be anywhere else? How many sweet words I should breathe into your ear, in the quiet night—how many holy kisses would I press upon your lips—whenever I…conscious of my bliss. But I should….

My little Dove, I have observed that butterflies—very broad-winged and magnificent butterflies, frequently come on board the salt ships where I am at work. What have these bright strangers to do on Long Wharf, where there are no flowers nor any green thing—nothing but brick stores, stone piers, black ships, and the bustle of toilsome men, who neither look up to the blue sky, nor take note of these wandering gems in the air.

I cannot account for them, unless, dearest, they are the lovely fantasies of your mind, which you send thither in search of me. There is the supper bell. Good bye, darling.

Sept 25th, morning—Dove, I have but a single moment to embrace you. Tell Sophie Hawkins I love her.

Husband,
Nathaniel

~~*

Nathaniel Hathorne (1804–1864) was a popular American romantic writer, most remembered for his classic novels, *The Scarlett Letter* and *The House of the Seven Gables*. He also wrote the successful campaign biography of his friend, President Franklin Pierce.

Hawthorne courted Elizabeth Peabody, who introduced him to her sister, Sophia. They became engaged in 1838 and he joined a transcendentalist Utopian community to save money so they could marry, which they finally did in 1842. They had three children, and lived as a happily married couple until he died in his sleep.

Sophia wrote of her husband, "I am always so dazzled and bewildered with the richness, the depth, the jewels of beauty in his productions that I am always looking forward to a second reading where I

can ponder and muse and fully take in the miraculous
wealth of thoughts."

Inside cover of *Frankenstein; or, The Modern
Prometheus* by Mary Shelley (1831)

Percy Bysshe Shelley

to Mary Wollstonecraft Godwin

October 27, 1813
Cumbria, England

Oh my dearest love why are our pleasures so short and so uninterrupted? How long is this to last? Know you my best Mary that I feel myself in your absence almost degraded to the level of the vulgar and impure.

I feel their vacant stiff eyeballs fixed upon me—until I seem to have been infected with a loathsome meaning... to inhale a sickness that subdues me to languor. Oh! those redeeming eyes of Mary that they might beam upon me before I sleep!

Praise my forbearance oh beloved one that I do not rashly fly to you... and at least secure a moment's bliss—Wherefore should I delay ... do you not long to meet me? All that is exalted and buoyant in my nature urges me towards you... reproaches me with cold delay... laughs at all fear and spurns to dream of prudence! Why am I not with you?—Alas we must not meet.

~~*

Percy Bysshe Shelley (1792–1822) was one of the finest English romantic poets. Much idolized by later generations, he is most remembered for his lyric anthologies *Ozymandias* and *Ode to the West Wind*, and his masterpiece, *Prometheus Unbound*. At nineteen his second wife, Mary Shelley, wrote the first science fiction novel, *Frankenstein*.

Shelley married a sixteen year old Harriet Westbrook in August 1811. Two years later he became a follower of political philosopher William Godwin, frequently visiting Godwin's home and bookshop in London, where he met and fell in love with Godwin's daughter, Mary Wollstonecraft Godwin, who would later become famous as Mary Shelley. In July 1814, Shelley abandoned his pregnant wife and baby daughter and ran away with Mary. The pair lived footloose but were ostracized and hounded by creditors. When Harriet committed suicide, Percy and Mary were married in late 1816.

The following year, the newlyweds spent the summer with Lord Byron in Geneva, where Mary conceived the idea for her pioneer gothic novel in a ghost story contest among the young writers. Percy tragically drowned when his sailboat went down in a storm in the Bay of Spezia in 1822. Mary returned to England, devoting herself to writing and raising their son.

Robert Browning

to Elizabeth Moulton Barrett

1845
Surrey, England

I love your verses with all my heart, dear Miss Barrett,—and this is no off–hand complimentary letter that I shall write,—whatever else, no prompt matter-of-course recognition of your genius and there a graceful and natural end of the thing: since the day last week when I first read your poems, I quite laugh to remember how I have been turning and turning again in my mind what I should be able to tell you of their effect upon me—for in the first flush of delight I thought I would this once get out of my habit of purely passive enjoyment, when I do really enjoy, and thoroughly justify my admiration—perhaps even, as a loyal fellow craftsman should, try and find fault and do you some little good to be proud of hereafter!—but nothing comes of it all—so into me has it gone, and part of me has it become, this great living poetry of your, not a flower of which but took root and grew... oh, how different that is from lying to be dried and pressed flat and prized highly and put in a book with a proper account at top and bottom, and shut up and put away... and the book called a 'Flora', besides!

After all, I need not give up the thought of doing that, too, in time; because even now, talking with whoever is worthy, I can give a reason form my faith in one and another excellence, the fresh strange music, the affluent language, the exquisite pathos and true new brave thought—but in this addressing myself to you, your own self, and for the first time, my feeling rises altogether.

I do, as I say, love these Books with all my heart—
and I love you too; do you know I was once not very
far from seeing—really seeing you? Mr. Kenyon
said to me one morning "would you like to see Miss
Barrett?"—then he went to announce me,—then he
returned... you were too unwell—and now it is years
ago—and I feel as at some untoward passage in my
travels—as if I had been close, so close, to some
world's–wonder in chapel or crypt,... only a screen
to push and I might have entered—but there was
some slight... so it now seems... slight and just-
sufficient bar to admission, and the half-opened door
shut, and I went home my thousands of miles, and the
sight was never to be!

Well, these Poems were to be—and this true
thankful joy and pride with which I feel myself.

Yours ever faithfully
Robert Browning

~~*

Robert Browning (1812–1889) was a preeminent
Victorian romantic poet, most remembered for his
collection of poems *Men and Women*, inspired by and
dedicated to his wife, the poet Elizabeth Barrett
Browning. His exquisitely crafted dramatic
monologues heavily influenced subsequent literary
generations.

After reading the popular and acclaimed poems of
Elizabeth Moulton Barrett, a thirty-nine year old
semi-invalid spinster still living with her domineering
father, Robert began to correspond with her.
Through their writing the two developed a deep
romantic attachment, and secretly eloped to Italy the
following year. They had a son, Robert "Pen"
Browning, in 1849 and lived together happily until
Elizabeth's untimely death in 1861.

Robert inspired Elizabeth to write her autobiographical masterpiece, *Sonnets from the Portuguese*, which famously begins, "How do I love thee? Let me count the ways."

Gustave Flaubert

to Louise Colet

August 9, 1846
Croisset, France

I embrace you, I kiss you. I feel wild. Were you here, I'd bite you; I long to do so—I, whom, women jeer at for my coldness—I, charitably supposed to be incapable of sex, so little have I indulged in it.

Yet, I feel within me now the appetites of wild beasts, the instincts of a love that is carnivorous, capable of tearing flesh to pieces. Is this love?

Perhaps it is the opposite. Perhaps in my case it's the heart that is impotent.

August 15, 1846
I will cover you with love when next I see you, with caresses, with ecstasy. I want to gorge you with all the joys of the flesh, so that you faint and die. I want you to be amazed by me, and to confess to yourself that you had never even dreamed of such transports... When you are old, I want you to recall those few hours, I want your dry bones to quiver with joy when you think of them.

August 1846
Adieu, I seal my letter, this is the hour when, alone amidst everything that sleeps, I open the drawer that holds my treasures. I look at your slippers, your handkerchief, your hair, your portrait. I re-read your letters, and breathe their musky perfume.

If you could know what I am feeling at this moment! My heart expands in the night, penetrated by a dew of love!

~~*

Gustave Flaubert (1821–1880) was one of the foremost French writers, best known for his classic novel, *Madame Bovary*, a groundbreakingly honest portrait of life that remains the pinnacle of literary realism.

Flaubert lived with his mother and never married. Though a known user of local courtesans, from whom he contracted the disease that would eventually lead to his demise, his only serious romantic relationship was a torrid eight-year love affair with married poet Louise Colet that began in 1846 when she was thirty-five.

The Pit and the Pendulum by Harry Clarke from
Tales of Mystery and Imagination
by Edgar Allan Poe (1919)

Edgar Allen Poe

to Sarah Helen Whitman

October 1, 1848
The Bronx, New York

I cannot better explain to you what I felt than by saying that your unknown heart seemed to pass into my bosom—there to dwell forever—while mine, I thought, was translated into your own.

From that hour I loved you. Yes, I now feel that it was then—on that evening of sweet dreams—that the very first dawn of human love burst upon the icy night of my spirit. Since that period I have never seen nor heard your name without a shiver half of delight, half of anxiety... for years your name never past my lips, while my soul drank in, with a delirious thirst, all that was uttered in my presence respecting you.

The merest whisper that concerned you awoke in me a shuddering sixth sense, vaguely compounded of fear, ecstatic happiness, and a wild, inexplicable sentiment that resembled nothing so nearly as the consciousness of guilt.

~~*

Edgar Allan Poe (1809–1849) was an American poet and short-story writer, best known for his tales of mystery and the macabre, including *The Fall of the House of Usher, The Pit and the Pendulum,* and his popular poetic masterpiece, *The Raven.* He also influenced the field of cryptography, the burgeoning new art form of science fiction, and invented the genre of detective fiction.

At age twenty-seven Edgar married his thirteen year old cousin, Virginia Clemm, who idolized him. He too was happy and devoted, saying, "I see no one among the living as beautiful as my little wife." She began struggling with consumption in 1842 and died from it five years later, plummeting him into severe depression and alcoholism.

Edgar first saw poet Sarah Helen Power Whitman—a widow six years his elder—in 1845, standing in a rose garden behind her house, but declined to meet her. Later, a year after his wife's death, Sarah wrote a Valentine's Day poem dedicated *To Edgar Allan Poe*, and he reciprocated by writing the poem *To Helen*, about the moment he first laid eyes on her.

Sharing many common interests, the two exchanged letters and poetry and traveled between New York and Providence to meet. In late 1848 they became engaged, but the wedding was called off at the insistence of her mother due to his drinking, which the breakup worsened. Within a year he was dead.

Late Nineteenth Century

Count Leo Tolstoy

to Valeria Arsenev

November 2, 1856
Saint Petersburg

I already love in you your beauty, but I am only beginning to love in you that which is eternal and ever precious—your heart, your soul.

Beauty one could get to know and fall in love with in one hour and cease to love it as speedily; but the soul one must learn to know.

Believe me, nothing on earth is given without labour, even love, the most beautiful and natural of feelings.

~~*

Count Lev Nikolayevich Tolstoi (1828–1910) was a Russian writer, widely regarded as one of history's greatest novelists, most remembered for his mammoth masterworks of realism, *War and Peace* and *Anna Karenina.* He also founded a school for peasant children. His command service in the Crimean War led him to become a pacifist in later life, and his principals of nonviolent resistance inspired Mahatma Gandi and Martin Luther King Jr.

Tolstoy described his early life thus. "I put men to death in war, I fought duels to slay others. I lost at cards, wasted the substance wrung from the sweat of peasants, punished the latter cruelly, rioted with loose women, and deceived men. Lying, robbery, adultery of all kinds, drunkenness, violence, and murder, all were committed by me, not one crime omitted, and yet I was not the less considered by my equals to be a comparatively moral man. Such was my life for ten years."

In 1856, shortly after leaving the army and the loss of his brother to tuberculosis, Tolstoy courted and became engaged to the beautiful Valeria Arsenev. However—wanting her to understand him completely before marriage—he gave her his diaries; the shock ended their relationship.

Though Tolstoy believed no woman could love him, six years later he married his friend's sister, nineteen year old Sofia Andreyevna Behrs. His beloved Sonya bore him more than a dozen children over their many blissful and prosperous years together.

Balzac

to Ewelina Hańska

June 19, 1836
Paris

Sunday 19th
My beloved angel,

—I am nearly mad about you, as much as one can be mad: I cannot bring together two ideas that you do not interpose yourself between them.

I can no longer think of anything but you. In spite of myself, my imagination carries me to you. I grasp you, I kiss you, I caress you, a thousand of the most amorous caresses take possession of me.

As for my heart, there you will always be—very much so. I have a delicious sense of you there. But my God, what is to become of me, if you have deprived me of my reason? This is a monomania which, this morning, terrifies me.

I rise up every moment saying to myself, "Come, I am going there!" Then I sit down again, moved by the sense of my obligations. There is a frightful conflict. This is not life. I have never before been like that. You have devoured everything.

I feel foolish and happy as soon as I think of you. I whirl round in a delicious dream in which in one instant I live a thousand years. What a horrible situation!

Overcome with love, feeling love in every pore, living only for love, and seeing oneself consumed by griefs, and caught in a thousand spiders' threads.

O, my darling Eva, you did not know it. I picked up your card. It is there before me, and I talk to you as if you were there. I see you, as I did yesterday, beautiful, astonishingly beautiful.

Yesterday, during the whole evening, I said to myself "she is mine!" Ah! The angels are not as happy in Paradise as I was yesterday!

~~*

Honoré de Balzac (1799–1850) was a French playright and novelist best remembered for his massive collective masterpiece of realism, *The Human Comedy*, which greatly influenced future generations of authors and philosophers. He is the subject of a monument by sculptor Auguste Rodin.

Balzac suffered from health problems throughout his life, possibly due to his intense writing schedule. His relationship with his family was often strained by financial and personal drama,

In 1832, Balzac received a letter with no return address signed The Foreigner, commenting on one of his works. He replied by classified advertisement in the *Gazette de France*, beginning a lifelong correspondence with "the object of his sweetest dreams," Ewelina Rzewuska Hańska, who was trapped in an arranged marriage to a wealthy man twenty years her elder. When her husband died in 1841, he came to her and they became paramours. Shortly before his death, they finally married.

Lithograph of Robert and Clara Schumann in
Vienna (1847)

Robert Schumann

to Clara Wieck

1838
Leipzig, Germany

What a heavenly morning!   All the bells are ringing; the sky is so golden and clear... and before me lays your letter.

I send you my first kiss, beloved.

1838
Leipzig

Clara,

How happy your last letters have made me—those since Christmas Eve! I should like to call you by all the endearing epithets, and yet I can find no lovelier word than the simple word "dear," but there is a particular way of saying it. My dear one, then, I have wept for joy to think that you are mine, and often wonder if I deserve you.

One would think that no one man's heart and brain could stand all the things that are crowded into one day. Where do these thousands of thoughts, wishes, sorrows, joys and hopes come from? Day in, day out, the procession goes on. But how light-hearted I was yesterday and the day before! There shone out of your letters so noble a spirit, such faith, such a wealth of love!

What would I not do for love of you, my own Clara! The knights of old were better off; they could go through fire or slay dragons to win their ladies, but we of today have to content ourselves with more prosaic methods, such as smoking fewer cigars, and the like. After all, though, we can love, knights or no knights; and so, as ever, only the times change, not men's hearts...

You cannot think how your letter has raised and strengthened me... You are splendid, and I have much more reason to be proud of you than you of me. I have made up my mind, though, to read all your wishes in your face. Then you will think, even though you don't say it, that your Robert is a really good sort, that he is entirely yours, and he loves you more than words can say.

You shall indeed have cause to think so in the happy future. I still see you as you looked in your little cap that last evening. I still hear you call me du. Clara, I heard nothing of what you said but that du. Don't you remember?

But I see you in many another unforgettable guise. Once you were in a black dress, going to the theatre with Emilia List; it was during our separation. I know you will not have forgotten; it is vivid with me. Another time you were walking in the Thomasgasschen with an umbrella up, and you avoided me in desperation. And yet another time, as you were putting on your hat after a concert, our eyes happened to meet, and yours were full of the old unchanging love.

I picture you in all sorts of ways, as I have seen you since. I did not look at you much, but you charmed me so immeasurably... Ah, I can never praise you enough for yourself or for your love of me, which I don't really deserve.

Robert

~~*

Robert Alexander Schumann (1810–1856) was a famous German romantic composer, married to superstar virtuoso pianist Clara Josephine Wieck Schumann.

Clara was the daughter of Robert's teacher, Friedrich Wieck, who believed his student could become a virtuoso before an unfortunate hand injury. By 1836, Robert and Clara were madly in love, and the following year he asked her father for her hand in marriage. Overprotective Friedrich was strenuously opposed to the relationship, and they were forced to fight a long and bitter legal battle for court permission to marry, finally wedding in 1840 and living happily thereafter.

Throughout her six decade concert career as "the high priestess of music," Clara showcased many of her husband's works, including his deceptively simple *The Dream*, one of the most famous piano pieces ever written.

Major Sullivan Ballou

to Sarah Ballou

July the 14th, 1861
Washington, D.C.

My very dear Sarah:

The indications are very strong that we shall move in a few days—perhaps tomorrow. Lest I should not be able to write you again, I feel impelled to write lines that may fall under your eye when I shall be no more.

Our movement may be one of a few days duration and full of pleasure—and it may be one of severe conflict and death to me. Not my will, but thine O God, be done. If it is necessary that I should fall on the battlefield for my country, I am ready. I have no misgivings about, or lack of confidence in, the cause in which I am engaged, and my courage does not halt or falter. I know how strongly American Civilization now leans upon the triumph of the Government, and how great a debt we owe to those who went before us through the blood and suffering of the Revolution. And I am willing—perfectly willing—to lay down all my joys in this life, to help maintain this Government, and to pay that debt.

But, my dear wife, when I know that with my own joys I lay down nearly all of yours, and replace them in this life with cares and sorrows—when, after having eaten for long years the bitter fruit of orphanage myself, I must offer it as their only sustenance to my dear little children—is it weak or dishonourable, while the banner of my purpose floats calmly and proudly in the breeze, that my unbounded love for you, my darling wife and children, should struggle in fierce, though useless, contest with my love of country?

I cannot describe to you my feelings on this calm summer night, when two thousand men are sleeping around me, many of them enjoying the last, perhaps, before that of death—and I, suspicious that Death is creeping behind me with his fatal dart, am communing with God, my country, and thee.

I have sought most closely and diligently, and often in my breast, for a wrong motive in thus hazarding the happiness of those I loved and I could not find one. A pure love of my country and of the principles have often advocated before the people and "the name of honour that I love more than I fear death" have called upon me, and I have obeyed.

Sarah, my love for you is deathless, it seems to bind me to you with mighty cables that nothing but Omnipotence could break; and yet my love of Country comes over me like a strong wind and bears me irresistibly on with all these chains to the battlefield.

The memories of the blissful moments I have spent with you come creeping over me, and I feel most gratified to God and to you that I have enjoyed them so long. And hard it is for me to give them up and burn to ashes the hopes of future years, when God willing, we might still have lived and loved together and seen our sons grow up to honourable manhood around us. I have, I know, but few and small claims upon Divine Providence, but something whispers to me—perhaps it is the wafted prayer of my little Edgar—that I shall return to my loved ones unharmed. If I do not, my dear Sarah, never forget how much I love you, and when my last breath escapes me on the battlefield, it will whisper your name.

Forgive my many faults, and the many pains I have caused you. How thoughtless and foolish I have oftentimes been! How gladly would I wash out with my tears every little spot upon your happiness, and struggle with all the misfortune of this world, to shield you and my children from harm. But I cannot. I must watch you from the spirit land and hover near you, while you buffet the storms with your precious little freight, and wait with sad patience till we meet to part no more.

But, O Sarah! If the dead can come back to this earth and flit unseen around those they loved, I shall always be near you; in the garish day and in the darkest night—amidst your happiest scenes and gloomiest hours—always, always; and if there be a soft breeze upon your cheek, it shall be my breath; or the cool air fans your throbbing temple, it shall be my spirit passing by.

Sarah, do not mourn me dead; think I am gone and wait for thee, for we shall meet again.

As for my little boys, they will grow as I have done, and never know a father's love and care. Little Willie is too young to remember me long, and my blue-eyed Edgar will keep my frolics with him among the dimmest memories of his childhood. Sarah, I have unlimited confidence in your maternal care and your development of their characters. Tell my two mothers his and hers I call God's blessing upon them. O Sarah, I wait for you there! Come to me, and lead thither my children.

Sullivan

~~*

Sullivan Ballou (1829–1861), was a lawyer and politician, and major in the Second Regiment of the

Rhode Island Volunteers during the American Civil War.

Ballou wrote the above letter to his wife Sarah from a military camp outside the capital, a week before he fought—and died—in the first major engagement of the war, the Battle of Bull Run.

More than a century later his words were featured on a public television documentary about the Civil War, and they came to symbolize the struggles and sacrifice of every American who fought to end slavery and preserve the Union.

Mark Twain

to Olivia Langdon

1869
Buffalo, New York

Livy dear,

I have already mailed today's letter, but I am so proud of my privilege of writing the dearest girl in the world whenever I please, that I must add a few lines if only to say I love you, Livy. For I do love you, Livy... as the dew loves the flowers; as the birds love the sunshine; as the wavelets love the breeze; as mothers love their first-born; as memory loves old faces; as the yearning tides love the moon; as the angels love the pure in heart... Take my kiss and my benediction, and try to be reconciled to the fact that I am

Yours forever,
Sam

P.S.—I have read this letter over and it is flippant and foolish and puppyish. I wish I had gone to bed when I got back, without writing. You said I must never tear up a letter after writing it to you and so I send it. Burn it, Livy, I did not think I was writing so clownishly and shabbily. I was in much too good a humor for sensible letter writing.

May 12, 1869

Out of the depths of my happy heart wells a great tide of love and prayer for this priceless treasure that is confided to my life–long keeping.

You cannot see its intangible waves as they flow towards you, darling, but in these lines you will hear, as it were, the distant beating of the surf.

~~*

Samuel Langhorne Clemens (1835–1910), better known as Mark Twain, is considered the father of American literature, most remembered for his classic American novel, *Adventures of Huckleberry Finn*, and its sequel *The Adventures of Tom Sawyer*. His keen wit made him immensely popular with the social elite and the general public alike.

It was love at first sight when Twain met Olivia Langdon, who came from a wealthy but liberal family. They were engaged within a year, and married in 1870. Their love and marriage lasted thirty-four years until her death.

The Starry Night by Vincent van Gogh (1889)

Vincent Van Gogh

to Theo van Gogh

November 3, 1881
Etten, The Netherlands

Dear Theo,

There is something on my mind that I want to tell you about. You may perhaps know something of it already and it will not be news to you. I wanted to let you know that I fell so much in love with Kee Vos this summer that I can find no other words for it than, "It is just as if Kee Vos were the closest person to me and I the closest person to Kee Vos," and—those words I spoke to her. But when I told her this, she replied that her past and her future remained as one to her so that she could never return my feelings.

Then I was in a tremendous dilemma about what to do. Should I resign myself to that "never, no, never," or consider the matter not yet settled and done with, keep in good heart and not give up?

I chose the latter. And to this day I do not regret this approach, although I am still up against that "never, no, never." Since then, of course, I have had to put up with quite a few "life's little troubles" which, had they been written about in a book, might well have served to amuse some people, but which if one experiences oneself must be deemed anything but pleasant.

However, to this day I am glad that I left the resignation—or the "how not to do it" method—to those who have a mind for it and for myself kept in good heart. You will understand that in a case like this it is surprisingly difficult to tell what one can, may and must do. Yet "we pick up the scent as we wander about, not as we sit idly by."

One of the reasons I have not written to you about all this before is that my position was so uncertain and unsettled that I was unable to explain it to you. Now, however, we have reached the point where I have spoken about it, not only to her but to Father and Mother, to Uncle and Aunt Stricker and to our Uncle and Aunt at Prinsenhage.

The only one to say to me, and that very informally and privately, that there really might be a chance for me if I worked hard and made progress, was someone from whom I least expected it: Uncle Cent. He was pleased with the way in which I reacted to Kee's "never no, never," that is not making heavy weather of it but taking it in quite good humour, and said for instance, "Don't give grist to the never, no, never mills which Kee has set up, I wish her all the best, but I rather hope those mills will go bankrupt."

Similarly, I didn't take it amiss when Uncle Stricker said that there was the danger that I "might be severing friendly relationships and old ties." Whereupon I said that in my view the real issue, far from severing old ties, was to see if the old ones could not be renewed where they were in need of repair.

Anyway, that is what I hope to go on doing, and cast out despondency and gloom, meanwhile working hard—and ever since I met her, I have been getting on much better with my work.

I told you that the position has now become more clear cut. 1st.—Kee says "never, no, never" and then—I have the feeling that I'm going to have an immense amount of difficulty with the older people, who consider the matter settled and done with now and will try to force me to drop it.

For the time being, however, I think they'll go about it very gently, keeping me dangling and fobbing me off with fair words until Uncle and Aunt

Stricker's silver anniversary in December is over. I fear they will be taking measures to get rid of me.

Forgive me for expressing myself somewhat harshly in order to make the position clear to you. I admit that the colors are somewhat glaring and the lines somewhat starkly drawn, but that will give you a clearer insight into the affair than if I were to beat about the bush. So do not suspect me of lacking in respect for the older people.

However, I do believe that they are positively against it and I wanted to make that clear to you. They will try to make sure that Kee and I neither see or speak or write to each other, because they know very well that if we saw, spoke or wrote to each other, there would be a chance of Kee changing her mind. Kee herself thinks she will never change her mind, the older people are trying to convince me that she cannot change it, and yet they fear such a change.

The older people will change their minds about this affair, not when Kee changes her attitude but when I have become somebody who earns at least 1000 guilders a year. Once again, forgive me the hard contours with which I am outlining matters. If I receive a little sympathy from the older ones, I believe that some of the younger ones will be able to understand my position.

You may, Theo—you may hear it said of me that I want to force things, and expressions like that. Yet everyone knows how senseless force is in love. No, nothing is further from my thoughts.

But it is neither unfair nor unreasonable to wish that Kee and I, instead of not being allowed any contact with each other, might see, speak or write to each other so that we could come to know each other better, and even be able to tell whether or not we are suited to one another. A year of keeping in touch with each other would be salutary for her and for me, and yet the older people have really dug in their heels on this point. Were I rich, they would soon change their tune.

But now you will realize that I hope to leave no stone unturned that might bring me closer to her, and that is my intention:

To go on loving her

Until in the end she loves me too.

The more she disappears the more she appears.

Theo, are you by any chance in love as well? I hope you are, for believe me, even its "petites misères" have their value. One is sometimes in despair, there are moments when one is in hell, so to speak, yet there is also something different and better about it.

There are three stages.

1. Not loving and not being loved.
2. Loving and not being loved (the present case).
3. Loving and being loved.

Now, I tell you that the second stage is better than the first, but the third! That's it!

Well, old boy, go and fall in love yourself and tell me about it some time. Keep your own counsel in the present case and have some sympathy for me. Of course I would much rather have had a yea and amen, but I am almost pleased with my "never, no, never." (I take it for something, although older and wiser heads say it is nothing.)

Rappard has been here, and brought some watercolors that are coming on well. Mauve will be calling soon, I hope, otherwise I shall go to him. I am doing a good deal of drawing and have the feeling it is improving; I am working much more with the brush than before. It is so cold now that I do almost nothing but indoor figure-drawing, a seamstress, a basket-weaver, etc.

A handshake in my thoughts and write soon and believe me,
Ever yours,
Vincent

~~*

Vincent Willem van Gogh (1853–1890) was a Dutch expressionist painter widely considered to be the greatest artist who has ever lived. His drawings and paintings, including *Sunflowers, Irises, Saint–Remy*, and his magnum opus, *The Starry Night*, had enormous influence and are some of the world's best known, most popular and most expensive works.

While living in the Gelderland with his parents in the summer of 1881, Vincent spent his days painting and walking in the countryside with his cousin, Kee Vos–Stricker, a recently widowed single mother six years older than he. She rejected his proposal of marriage due to his inability to support himself financially, and refused ever to see him again. When Vincent held his hand over a lamp, saying, "Let me see her for as long as I can keep my hand in the flame," her father—his Uncle Stricker—blew out the flame.

Van Gogh was a tortured artist with a fondness for alcohol and absinthe, who cut off the lobe of his left ear during a seizure, and mortally shot himself in a field in 1890. His final words were, "the sadness will last forever."

Albumen photographic plate of Beatrice Hatch,
aged 7, by Lewis Carroll (1873)

Lewis Carroll

to Gertrude Chataway

October 28, 1876
Christ Church, Oxford

My Dearest Gertrude:
 You will be sorry, and surprised, and puzzled, to hear what a queer illness I have had ever since you went. I sent for the doctor, and said, "Give me some medicine, for I'm tired." He said, "Nonsense and stuff! You don't want medicine: go to bed!"
 I said, "No; it isn't the sort of tiredness that wants bed. I'm tired in the face." He looked a little grave, and said, "Oh, it's your nose that's tired: a person often talks too much when he thinks he knows a great deal." I said, "No, it isn't the nose. Perhaps it's the hair." Then he looked rather grave, and said, "Now I understand: you've been playing too many hairs on the pianoforte."
 "No, indeed I haven't!" I said, "and it isn't exactly the hair: it's more about the nose and chin." Then he looked a good deal graver, and said, "Have you been walking much on your chin lately?" I said, "No."
 "Well!" he said, "it puzzles me very much. Do you think it's in the lips?" "Of course!" I said. "That's exactly what it is!"
 Then he looked very grave indeed, and said, "I think you must have been giving too many kisses." "Well," I said, "I did give one kiss to a baby child, a little friend of mine."
 "Think again," he said; "are you sure it was only one?" I thought again, and said, "Perhaps it was eleven times." Then the doctor said, "You must not give her any more till your lips are quite rested again." "But what am I to do?" I said, "because you

~105~

see, I owe her a hundred and eighty-two more." Then he looked so grave that tears ran down his cheeks, and he said, "You may send them to her in a box."

Then I remembered a little box that I once bought at Dover, and thought I would someday give it to some little girl or other. So I have packed them all in it very carefully. Tell me if they come safe or if any are lost on the way."

to Mary Livock Mileham

6 September 1885
Eastbourne, England

Dearest May,
Thank you very much indeed for the peaches. They were delicious. Eating one was almost as nice as kissing you; Of course not quite; I think, if I had to give the exact measurement, I should say three— quarters as nice; We are having such a lovely time here; and the sands are beautiful. I only wish I could some day come across you, washing your pocket— handkerchief in a pool among the rocks? But I wander on the beach, and look for you, in vain; and then I say, "Where is May?" And the stupid boatmen reply, "It isn't May, sir? It's September?" But it doesn't comfort me.
Always your Loving
C.L.D.

~~*

The Reverend Charles Lutwidge Dodgson (1832–1898), better known as Lewis Carroll, was an English mathematician and author, most remembered for his ground-breaking children's story, *Alice's Adventures in Wonderland* and its sequel *Through the Looking Glass*, as well as the epic poem Jabberwocky. His deftness at logic and word play challenged many Victorian era preconceptions and continues to influence modern culture.

Carroll met his child friend, Gertrude Chataway, while on seaside holiday when she was nine years old, and continued to write to and spend holidays with her until she was in her late twenties. She inspired his nonsense epic, *The Hunting of the Snark*, which is dedicated to her.

Carroll met Mary Livock Mileham wandering on the beach when she was ten years old, and saw her frequently until Mary's parents broke off their friendship two years later.

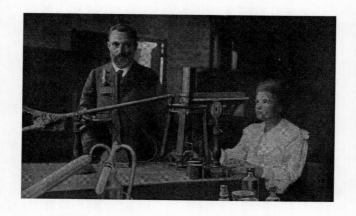

Newspaper photograph of Pierre and Marie Curie
in their laboratory (1905)

Pierre Curie

to Maria Skłodowska

August 10, 1894
Paris

Nothing could have given me greater pleasure that to receive news of you. The prospect of remaining two months without hearing about you had been extremely disagreeable to me: that is to say, your little note was more than welcome.

I hope you are laying up a stock of good air and that you will come back to us in October. As for me, I think I will not go anywhere; I will stay in the country, where I spend the whole day in front of my open window or in the garden.

We have promised each other—have we not?—to be at least great friends. If only you will not change your mind. For there are no promises that are binding; such things cannot be ordered at will. It would be a fine thing, just the same, in which I hardly dare believe, to pass our lives near each other, hypnotized by our dreams: your patriotic dream, our humanitarian dream, and our scientific dream.

Of all those dreams the last is, I believe, the only legitimate one. I mean by that that we are powerless to change the social order and, even if we were not, we should not know what to do; in taking action, no matter in what direction, we should never be sure of not doing more harm than good, by retarding some inevitable evolution. From the scientific point of view, on the contrary, we may hope to do something; the ground is more solid here, and any discovery that we may make, however small, will remain acquired knowledge.

See how it works out: it is agreed that we shall be great friends, but if you leave France in a year it would be an altogether too platonic friendship, that of two creatures who would never see each other again. Would it not be better for you to stay with me? I know that this question angers you, and that you do not want to speak of it again—and then, too, I feel so thoroughly unworthy of you from every point of view.

I thought of asking your permission to meet you by chance in Fribourg. But you are staying there, unless I am mistaken, only one day, and on that day you will of course belong to our friends the Kovalskis.

Believe me your very devoted
Pierre Curie

~~*

Pierre Curie (1859—1906) was a French physicist and pioneer in electromagnetism and radioactivity. He shared the 1903 Nobel Prize in physics with his Polish wife, Madame Maria Skłodowska Curie, who later won a second Nobel Prize in chemistry—the only person ever to do so. Their daughter, Irène Joliot-Curie, was also a Nobel laureate.

While an instructor at the Paris Institute of Technology, Pierre met a young doctoral student who had graduated first in her class from the Sorbonne. Their mutual interest in magnetism, appropriately enough, drew them together. Though he was smitten and begged her to stay, Maria returned to Warsaw for the summer and applied for a position at Kraków University. When she was rejected because she was a woman, she returned to Paris, and Pierre. They were married the following year—living, working, and traveling together from then on.

Pierre was tragically killed in a street accident a decade later, devastating Marie, who later had a scandalous affair with a married colleague. Though she founded the Curie Institute and the Maria Skłodowska-Curie Institute of Oncology, and was the first female professor at the University of Paris, the French Academy of Sciences refused her membership because of her gender.

George Bernard Shaw

to Ellen Terry

June 14, 1897
Surrey, England

The midnight train—gets to Dorking at 1 (a.m.) 14th-15th June 1897—stopping just now, but will joggle like mad presently

Do you read these jogged scrawls, I wonder. I think of your poor eyes, and resolve to tear what I have written up: then I look out at the ghostly country and the beautiful night, and I cannot bring myself to read a miserable book... Yes, as you guess, Ellen, I am having a bad attack of you just at present. I am restless; and a man's restlessness always means a woman; and my restlessness means Ellen. And your conduct is often shocking. Today I was wandering somewhere...when I glanced at a shop window; and there you were—oh disgraceful and abandoned—in your third Act Sans Gene dress—a mere waistband—laughing wickedly, and saying maliciously: "Look have restless one, at your pillow, at what you are really thinking about." How can you look Window and Grove's camera in the face with such thoughts in your head and almost nothing on...

Oh fie, fie, let me get away from this stuff, which you have been listening to all your life, & despise— though indeed, dearest Ellen, these silly longings stir up great waves of tenderness in which there is no guile.

I shall find a letter from you when I get back to Lotus, shall I not? Reigate we are at now; and it's a quarter to one. In ten minutes, Dorking station; in seventeen minutes thereafter, Lotus, and a letter. Only a letter, perhaps not even that. O Ellen, what will you say when the Recording Angel asks you why one of your sins have my name to them?

~~*

George Bernard Shaw (1856–1950) was an Irish playwright best remembered for *Pygmalion*—that the award-winning *My Fair Lady* is based on. Like a true modern fian, he was born into an impoverished branch of the Irish landed gentry. He is the only person to have been awarded both the Nobel Prize for Literature and an Oscar.

Ellen Terry was the most celebrated actress of her generation. After several relationships and two broken marriages, she began a famous "paper courtship" with Shaw.

Shaw was married to Charlotte Payne-Townshend, and accepted his Nobel Prize at her behest: she considered it a tribute to Ireland. He died at age 94, attributing his longevity to his vegetarian lifestyle.

Photograph of Jack London on Sonoma Mountain
(1914)

Twentieth Century

Jack London

to Anna Strunsky

April 3, 1901
Oakland, California

Dear Anna:

Did I say that the human might be filed in categories? Well, and if I did, let me qualify—not all humans. You elude me. I cannot place you, cannot grasp you. I may boast that of nine out of ten, under given circumstances, I can forecast their action; that of nine out of ten, by their word or action, I may feel the pulse of their hearts. But of the tenth I despair. It is beyond me. You are that tenth.

Were ever two souls, with dumb lips, more incongruously matched! We may feel in common— surely, we oftimes do—and when we do not feel in common, yet do we understand; and yet we have no common tongue. Spoken words do not come to us. We are unintelligible. God must laugh at the mummery.

The one gleam of sanity through it all is that we are both large temperamentally, large enough to often understand. True, we often understand but in vague glimmering ways, by dim perceptions, like ghosts, which, while we doubt, haunt us with their truth. And still, I, for one, dare not believe; for you are that tenth which I may not forecast.

Am I unintelligible now? I do not know. I imagine so. I cannot find the common tongue.

Large temperamentally—that is it. It is the one thing that brings us at all in touch. We have, flashed through us, you and I, each a bit of universal, and so we draw together. And yet we are so different.

I smile at you when you grow enthusiastic? It is a forgivable smile— nay, almost an envious smile. I have lived twenty-five years of repression. I learned not to be enthusiastic. It is a hard lesson to forget. I begin to forget, but it is so little. At the best, before I die, I cannot hope to forget all or most. I can exult, now that I am learning, in little things, in other things; but of my things, and secret things doubly mine, I cannot, I cannot. Do I make myself intelligible? Do you hear my voice? I fear not. There are poseurs. I am the most successful of them all.

Jack

~~*

Jack London (1876–1916) was America's first professional writer with a lucrative career in popular fiction, best known for *The Call of the Wild*, and other books—as well as commercial magazine fiction—concerning his many outdoor adventures.

At the turn of the century, he married Bessie Maddern, with whom he had a son and daughter, though publicly acknowledging they were marrying, not out of love, but from friendship and a belief that they would produce sturdy children. They divorced after four declining years of marriage.

Shortly after the honeymoon ended, London started an affair with Anna Strunsky that he maintained throughout the marriage, co-authoring *The Kempton-Wace Letters*, in which Anna's character argues for a romantic view of marriage. Jack's argues for a scientific view, contrasting two women he has known, "a mad, wanton creature, wonderful and unmoral and filled with life to the brim. My blood pounds hot even now as I conjure her up" and "a proud-breasted woman, the perfect mother, made preeminently to know the lip clasp of a child. You know the kind, the type."

A year after divorcing "Mother-Girl" Bess, London married Charmian Kittredge, the secretary of his MacMillan Publisher. Charmian was Jack's soulmate, always at his side on their numerous trips to exotic destinations like Hawaii and Australia.

London was an outspoken racist and avowed Socialist. He died of an accidental morphine overdose on the sleeping porch of his ranch house in 1916.

Photograph of Peary sledge from *The North Pole:*
Its Discovery in 1909 Under the Auspices
of the Peary Arctic Club (1910)

Admiral Peary

to Josephine Peary

August 17, 1908
S.S. *Roosevelt,*

My Darling Josephine:
  Am nearly through with my writing. Am brain weary with the thousand and one imperative details and things to think of. Everything thus far has gone well, too well I am afraid, and I am (solely on general principles) somewhat suspicious of the future. The ship is in better shape than before; the party and crew are apparently harmonious; I have 21 Eskimo men (against 23 last time) but the total of men women and children is only 50 as against 67 before owing to a more careful selection as to children... I have landed supplies here, and leave two men ostensibly on behalf of Cook.
  As a matter of fact I have established here the sub-base which last I established at Victoria Head, as a precaution in event of loss of the *Roosevelt* either going up this fall or coming down next summer. In some respects this is an advantage as on leaving here there is nothing to delay me or keep me from taking either side of the Channel going up. The conditions give me entire control of the situation...
  You have been with me constantly, sweetheart. At Kangerdlooksoah I looked repeatedly at Ptarmigan Island and thought of the time we camped there. At Nuuatoksoah I landed where we were. And on the 11th we passed the mouth of Bowdoin Bay in brilliant weather, and as long as I could I kept my eyes on Anniversary Lodge. We have been great chums dear. Tell Marie to remember what I told her, tell "Mister Man" to remember "straight and strong

and clean and honest," obey orders, and never forget that Daddy put "Mut" in his charge till he himself comes back to take her. In fancy I kiss your dear eyes and lips and cheeks sweetheart; and dream of you and my children, and my home till I come again. Kiss my babies for me. Farewell.

Love, Love, Love. Your Bert

P.S. August 18, 9 a.m. ... Tell Marie that her fir pillow perfumes me to sleep.

~~*

Rear Admiral Robert Edwin Peary (1856–1920) was an American explorer who on April 6, 1909, together with African-American explorer Matthew Alexander Henson and four Inuits, was the first person to reach the North Pole.

Robert Peary had two children with his wife, Josephine Diebitsch Peary, a son, Robert Jr. ("Mister Man" in the letter), and a daughter, Marie. During their Arctic expeditions, both Peary and fellow explorer Henson fathered children with Inuit women. Peary had a second son, Kali, with his Inuit wife, Ally, with whom he began his relationship when she was just 14 years of age.

Expeditions to reach the geographic North Pole in 1900, 1902 and 1905 all ended in failure. For the final, Peary and 23 men set off from New York City aboard the Roosevelt on July 6, 1908. They wintered near Cape Sheridan on Ellesmere Island, and departed for the pole on February 28, 1909. In his diary for April 7, Peary wrote, "The Pole at last! The prize of 3 centuries, my dream and ambition for 23 years. Mine at last..."

He retired in 1911, and lived with his family in Eagle Island off the coast of Maine until his death nine years later.

Kafka

to Felice Bauer

November 11, 1912
Prague, Austria-Hungary

Fräulein Felice!

I am now going to ask you a favor which sounds quite crazy, and which I should regard as such, were I the one to receive the letter. It is also the very greatest test that even the kindest person could be put to. Well, this is it:

Write to me only once a week, so that your letter arrives on Sunday—for I cannot endure your daily letters, I am incapable of enduring them. For instance, I answer one of your letters, then lie in bed in apparent calm, but my heart beats through my entire body and is conscious only of you. I belong to you; there is really no other way of expressing it, and that is not strong enough. But for this very reason I don't want to know what you are wearing; it confuses me so much that I cannot deal with life; and that's why I don't want to know that you are fond of me. If I did, how could I, fool that I am, go on sitting in my office, or here at home, instead of leaping onto a train with my eyes shut and opening them only when I am with you? Oh, there is a sad, sad reason for not doing so. To make it short: My health is only just good enough for myself alone, not good enough for marriage, let alone fatherhood. Yet when I read your letter, I feel I could overlook even what cannot possibly be overlooked.

If only I had your answer now! And how horribly I torment you, and how I compel you, in the stillness of your room, to read this letter, as nasty a letter as has ever lain on your desk! Honestly, it strikes me sometimes that I prey like a spectre on your felicitous name! If only I had mailed Saturday's letter, in which I implored you never to write to me again, and in which I gave a similar promise. Oh God, what prevented me from sending that letter? All would be well. But is a peaceful solution possible now? Would it help if we wrote to each other only once a week? No, if my suffering could be cured by such means it would not be serious. And already I foresee that I shan't be able to endure even the Sunday letters. And so, to compensate for Saturday's lost opportunity, I ask you with what energy remains to me at the end of this letter: If we value our lives, let us abandon it all.

Did I think of signing myself Dein? No, nothing could be more false. No, I am forever fettered to myself, that's what I am, and that's what I must try to live with.

Franz

~~*

Franz Kafka (1883—1924) was one of the major German-language fiction writers of the 20th century, best known for *The Metamorphosis*. His unique body of writing, concerning troubled individuals in a nightmarishly impersonal and bureaucratic world, is among the most influential in Western literature.

In 1912, Kafka met Berlin dictaphone representative Felice Bauer at Austrian composer Max Brod's home. Over five tumultuous years they met occasionally, corresponded a great deal, and twice were engaged to be married. Their relationship finally ended in 1917, when he began to suffer from tuberculosis.

By 1921, Kafka developed an intense relationship with Czech journalist and writer Milena Jesenská, before finally succumbing to his ailments within a few years.

President Woodrow Wilson requests Declaration of
War from Special Session of Congress (1917)

Woodrow Wilson

to Edith Bolling Galt

September 19, 1915
The White House

My noble, incomparable Edith,

I do not know how to express or analyze the conflicting emotions that have surged like a storm through my heart all night long. I only know that first and foremost in all my thoughts has been the glorious confirmation you gave me last night—without effort, unconsciously, as of course—of all I have ever thought of your mind and heart.

You have the greatest soul, the noblest nature, the sweetest, most loving heart I have ever known, and my love, my reverence, my admiration for you, you have increased in one evening as I should have thought only a lifetime of intimate, loving association could have increased them.

You are more wonderful and lovely in my eyes than you ever were before; and my pride and joy and gratitude that you should love me with such a perfect love are beyond all expression, except in some great poem which I cannot write.

Your own,
Woodrow

~~*

Thomas Woodrow Wilson (1856–1924), 28th president of the United States, was an American statesman widely remembered for his high-minded idealism. After leading his country into World War I, he later created the League of Nations for which he was awarded the Nobel Peace Prize.

Wilson met Edith after the devastating 1914 death of his first wife, Ellen, with whom he had three daughters. Edith became First Lady of the United States when the two married in December 1915.

Wilson declared the first national Mother's Day in 1914 "on the second Sunday in May as a public expression of our love and reverence for the mothers of our country." During his second term in office the Nineteenth Amendment to the United States Constitution—giving women the right to vote—was passed and ratified. Wilson reluctantly gave his support, after suffragist Alice Paul's "Silent Sentinels" were incarcerated and tortured for the first political protest to picket the White House.

As wartime prosperity turned to postwar depression, Wilson collapsed with a debilitating stroke in 1919.

Connla and the Fairy Maiden from *Childhood's Favorites and Fairy Stories, Volume 1*, by various authors, including Woodrow Wilson, Theodore Roosevelt, Rudyard Kipling, and General Sir Robert Baden–Powell (1909)

Afterword

What's Past is Prologue
—Wm. Shakespeare, *The Tempest*

As Oscar Wilde said, the truth is rarely pure and never simple. It is perhaps not surprising how intensely men of great accomplishment can love the objects of their desires. What may be less expected is that puissance of raw emotion may correlate as easily to conjugal cataclysm as to happily ever after.

If psychoanalysts—such as the renowned Sigmund Freud—are correct, the opposite of love is not hate, but indifference. Men of greatness may be guilty of many things, but apathy is rarely one of them. Their love may turn to hate, or to despair, or to another;

those who love once may love again, often even more profoundly. Love is a powerful emotion, even more so in the psyches of powerful men.

Benjamin Franklin listed moderation among his thirteen virtues to live by, and said in his 1734 Poor Richard's Almanac, "Be temperate in wine, in eating, girls, and sloth," though he rarely followed his own advice. Franklin showed the same fierceness in his most personal correspondence as he did in his chosen vocation, a trait he shared with Roosevelt, Kipling, Shakespeare, Wilde, Freud, and many others. But that is another story: or, at least, another volume.

Index

2607848